Imperfectly Fierce & Focused

*Rising Above Your Imperfections
While Still Crushing Your Goals*

Keever Lernise Murdaugh
Visionary Author

Copyright © 2023 by Touched By A Dove Publishing

ALL RIGHTS RESERVED. No part of this book may be reproduced, distributed, or transmitted in any form, including photocopying, recording, or other electronic or mechanical methods without the prior written permission of the author or publisher, except as permitted by U.S. copyright law.

Book Editing by Dana M. Hutchinson
Cover Design by Shariva Smith
Interior Design and Layout by S. Michelle LeSuer

Library of Congress Cataloging – in – Publication Data: 2023913881

ISBN: 978-1-7355336-3-6

PRINTED IN THE UNITED STATES OF AMERICA

Table of Contents

Foreword   1

Introduction   9

Not Easily Broken   13
Keever Lernise Murdaugh

My Zig-Zag Journey   31
Amie Arizmendi

Confidence Trumps Perfectionism Every Time   51
Jacqueline Kaba-Harrison

Stay Out of the Trash   71
Fouchina Kirkendoll

Living Life to the Fullest: A Story of Passion, Perseverance, and Possibility   89
Omu Obilor

Breaking all the Rules   103
Lisa Dove Washington

To Conclude the Whole Matter...   117

Foreword

It is my great honor to introduce the anthology, *Imperfectly Fierce & Focused,* a collection of stories that celebrate the human spirit and the power of resilience, determination, and perseverance.

Life is unpredictable, and we all face challenges that threaten to derail us. But what sets the six phenomenal women who authored these stories apart from others was their ability to face their challenges head-on and find the strength to overcome them. Their personal testimonies demonstrate the strength and courage it took for them to keep going even when confronted with insurmountable odds.

They come from all walks of life and represent a wide range of experiences and perspectives. Some are established writers, while others are sharing their stories for the first time. But what united them all was their willingness to be vulnerable and share their struggles and triumphs with the hope to encourage others.

As you read their stories, you will be struck by the incredible diversity of experiences and the shared themes of courage, relentlessness, and humility. These are women who have faced poverty, divorce, miscarriages, addiction, illness, loss, and other significant setbacks, however they refused to let their challenges define them. These incredible women looked adversity square in the face and were determined to come out on the other side stronger than ever before.

One of the most inspiring things about this collaborative work is the way it challenges our cultural narrative of success. Too often, we are told that being successful is about achieving perfection, that we should always strive for more, and that anything less than is considered failure. But the authors share a different perspective, and that true success is more about embracing our imperfections and using them as strengths.

A must-read, *Imperfectly Fierce & Focused* also is a testament to the power of community and serves as a reminder that we're never alone. The authors, through their connections with others, found the support and encouragement they needed to keep going.

As I reflect on my own journey, I am reminded of the challenges I have faced and the lessons I learned along the way. Like many of the contributors, I have endured significant obstacles in my life, and there have been moments when I felt like giving up. But it was in those moments that I discovered just how strong and resilient I was.

Imperfectly Fierce & Focused is not just a collection of stories. It is a call to action, and a reminder that we all have the power to make a difference in the world. All of the authors in this compilation weren't afraid to show their "scars" if for no other reasons than to inspire and encourage others, create connections and build communities, and to be a force for good. With that being said, I challenge you to acknowledge and embrace your own imperfections that make you unique and allow yourself to be vulnerable by pouring into the lives of others, sharing your struggles and triumphs, and to be an example of what strength and resilience look like.

When we think of individuals who are fierce and focused, we often picture people who have it all together; are confident, self-assured, and seem to have life figured out. But the truth is, even the most successful and accomplished individuals are far from perfect. We all have flaws, insecurities, and moments of doubt and uncertainty.

That's what makes this book so inspiring. The authors come from all walks of life and represent a wide range of experiences and perspectives. Being vulnerable didn't come easy, of course. There were times, I'm sure when they felt like throwing in the towel and giving up. But they made a conscious decision to keep pushing forward, knowing that every step they took was bringing them closer to achieving their goals.

And that's the thing about being fierce and focused. It's not about being perfect or having it all together. It's about having the courage to keep going, even when things get tough. It's about being willing to take risks, being unafraid of making mistakes, but most importantly, making sure to learn from them. It's about believing in yourself, even when no one else does.

One of the writer's story resonated with me in particular. She chronicled an event in her life when her mom was in a near fatal car accident and their family lost EVERYTHING and had to move to the projects of South-Central Los Angeles. She also shared how she became pregnant at age 18, had a precious baby girl at age 19, received welfare and even served time, but today has made over $1M dollars, has three successful businesses, travels the world and lives the life she dreamed of. It's not about how you start, but how you finish!

In closing, I'm extremely grateful to all of the ladies who helped make this compilation a reality. Your stories are a source of inspiration and hope, and I am honored to be a part of this project. To all who add this published work to your library, you won't be disappointed.

Imperfectly,
Dr. Tina D. Lewis

Biography

Dr. Tina D. Lewis is a two-time Presidential Lifetime Achievement Award recipient (both received in 2022), a 10-time International Best-selling Author, and holds a Doctor of Philosophy degree with an emphasis in Entrepreneurship and Business Administration. She is also the CEO of Royalty Coaching LLC, a Strategic Marketing and Global Positioning firm. Most notably, she earned her first $100K in just 45 days and is affectionately known as "The Bottom-Line Queen."

The creator of The 6-Figure Incubator, Dr. Tina established this exclusive community to nurture entrepreneurs into becoming six-figure earners.

Recognized as a Certified Global Speaker, her messages are transformational. As a result, she founded Global Women Speakers, a professional organization that provides women the opportunity to share their messages, products, and services around the world. To learn more about this phenomenal organization and to become a member, go to www.GlobalWomenSpeakers.com.

FUN FACT: Dr. Tina has personally met Richard Branson, Donald Trump, and Oprah Winfrey!

Introduction

Have you ever struggled with imposter syndrome, procrastination or a false reality of perfection? Have you ever suffered from grief, trauma, abuse, anxiety or depression? Do you have a negative self-image or lack self-confidence? Have you ever received an unfavorable diagnosis or experienced relationship issues? With everything you're currently experiencing or have ever experienced, did you wonder how you were going to overcome or conquer them? Then wonder no more because I have just the solution for you.

I am Coach Keever L. Murdaugh, and I have the distinct pleasure as Visionary Author to introduce *Imperfectly Fierce & Focused: Rising Above Your Imperfections While Still Crushing Your Goals*. Life is clearly a journey. You never know what situations, trials, or tribulations that you will encounter. Nevertheless, it is important to look at each circumstance that you face with perspective and see the good out of each test. This anthology does just that! I, along with a group of amazing co-authors share personal testimonies of how we persevered and overcame indescribable odds.

This book is intended to reach those who are struggling to heal from trauma and depression, or who suffer from low self-esteem, lack self-confidence, or who are questioning their self-worth and/or resiliency primarily because of past insecurities. If that's you, it's time to get out of your own way. I was compelled to write this book with you in mind because as I've interacted with others from all walks of life, I've noticed a running parallel; that many were allowing the false reality of perfection to limit their progression in their personal and professional lives. They were crippled with fear of failure and judgment or struggled with stepping out of their comfort zones.

My prayer is, as you read *Imperfectly Fierce & Focused: Rising Above Your Imperfections While Still Crushing Your Goals,* you'll walk away not only feeling empowered, re-energized and inspired; but you'll also have an arsenal filled with tangible tips and strategies to implement immediately in your personal lives, businesses or relationships that will change your trajectory in a positive and productive way.

Keever L. Murdaugh
Visionary Author

"Never regret a day in your life. Good days bring you happiness and bad days bring you experience."
~Author unknown

"Nothing is impossible. The word itself says 'I'm possible.'"
~Audrey Hepburn

"What you are is God's gift to you, what you become is your gift to God."
~Hans urs von Balthasar

Not Easily Broken
Keever Lernise Murdaugh

The phrase "not easily broken" is sentimental to me for various reasons. It conveys strength, resiliency, commitment, tenacity, and courage. After hearing this phrase for the first time, I couldn't help but think about all that I have endured and overcome. I pray that by sharing my story, you will find the courage and strength to not allow anything, or anyone discourage you from giving up.

Growing up wasn't easy...

Like many, I did not have an easy life. Growing up I experienced poverty, domestic violence, moving from house to house, and at one point during my adult life I was even homeless. So I know about life's struggles first hand. However, I'm a firm believer that tests and trials happen to make us stronger. There are lessons in every struggle, traumatic experience, and time of sorrow. It's important to acknowledge and evaluate every situation that you face and to use them to teach others how to be survivors, more than conquerors, and victors.

I remember those years as if it were yesterday. We lived in a mobile home that was in dire need of repairs. There were soft spots and holes in the floors, with some of them under my bed. At night, I used to pray that my bed didn't fall through to the room below. And to add insult to injury, I had an abusive father. I remember so vividly the fights that he and my mother had regularly. The sounds of his fist connecting to her body and then her body hitting the walls still reverberates in my mind. Even now, those sounds still make me cringe and is something I may never overcome.

Despite how he treated her, she would always say, "Well, he is still your father, and you still have to respect him." Thinking back, I always wondered how she managed to find the strength to not hate or speak ill of him, especially with everything that he constantly put her through. He not only beat her, but he was a cheater and a liar. I often viewed her as a weak and timid woman. How dare she have the nerve to tell me to respect him just after getting beaten by him? Respect him, for what, for popping her in the mouth or giving her a black eye?

I could not wrap my young mind around what she was saying and why. However, it wasn't until I became an adult that I understood it. It took incredible strength for her not to instill in me and my sisters hatred towards him. She knew that eventually we would grow up and draw our own conclusions about him and she did not want to negatively influence us in any way. Oddly enough, in an attempt to get us to hate her, he would talk badly about her, the nerve! And that made me despise him even more. Our father did nothing for us, but our mom on the other hand worked two and sometimes three jobs to make ends meet, and yet he had the audacity to talk negatively about her.

However, every situation is a learning opportunity and I learned by watching my parents' volatile relationship and the relationship that my father had with me and my sisters, that I did not want the characteristics that he possessed in a man. I was determined not to be a statistic and I knew that I did not want to expose my future children to the mental, verbal, financial, and physical abuse that I endured as a child. I learned very early on how to identify red flags in a relationship and what I was and was not going to put up with. And if any man who I was dating remotely resembled my father's behavior in any way, I immediately ended the relationship. I was determined to break that generational curse and I did.

I love my father, but as a child he made it extremely hard to do so. He was spiteful and mean. I even had to beg him to attend my high school graduation, knowing just how much I wanted him to be there. You see, he never supported anything that I was involved in; not a basketball game, JROTC competition, parade ... nothing. So to have him experience the last major milestone of my high school career was monumental to me and to this day, he still refuses to give me the satisfaction of knowing if he was there to see me walk across the stage or not. For him to neither admit nor deny his presence bothered me for years.

It took me a long time just to forgive him and move on. Even though it has taken us years, we're now on semi-good terms and are making progress to strengthen our relationship. But thank God it is not what it used to be. As I stated earlier,

I love my father and he is the only one I have, so I have chosen to release the past and move forward because life is too short. We can be here today and gone tomorrow, so it's important to learn how to forgive, release the offense, and move forward. Even though I have forgiven him, I still remember the disappointments, hurt, and pain. The wounds have healed but the scars are still there. However, I am making strides towards wholeness every day.

Surviving, but not thriving...

As a young adult, life began to turn around. I graduated from high school at the top of my class, was the battalion commander of our Army JROTC program, was accepted into college, and was awarded a four-year Army scholarship. And to think, I was a child who came from humble beginnings. I was born with a speech impediment, living in poverty, witnessing my parents' toxic and abusive relationship, and lacking confidence.

Family can be your harshest critics. I was teased by my aunts and cousins because I did not act like everyone else in my family. I was often misunderstood simply because I was "different."

They called me "crack," a term used in the African American culture meaning that you don't have it all together mentally. I also stuttered and did not speak fluently like most, and it bothered me. However, I was given tools to help me with my speech impediment and the older I got the easier it became. As a child, I had no access to speech therapy, and I struggled. When I had something important to say, I used my middle sister as my mouth piece. She obliged me for a while, but eventually grew tired. At times I felt embarrassed when talking to people because I struggled with conveying my thoughts. It wasn't that I was slow or stupid, it was just that my brain processed my thoughts faster than I could get the words out.

When you are misunderstood, it can eat away at you. You tend to feel inadequate, unworthy, incompetent, useless, and so many other negative adjectives come to mind. But how many of you know that having a negative mindset is the trick of the enemy. Believe it or not, you were fearfully and wonderfully made. Every flaw was perfectly orchestrated by God. No one is like you and that alone is worth celebrating. Often we see our imperfections as weaknesses when in essence, they contribute to who we are.

When my family made fun of me, it did make me feel a certain way. To be honest, they are the type of people who will find something negative to say no matter what. Unfortunately, I allowed them to project their insecurities on me. However, in high school is where I began to find my voice and tap into my inner strength. Being involved in the JROTC program was when I learned that I was a natural born leader. When I spoke, people automatically stopped and listened. I could command a room and others were drawn to me.

I also learned that because of my strength, not everyone knew how to handle it, including me at times. I was often told that I was too much. I know, right? The irony of it all was apparent. I literally went from a poor, shy kid, who lacked confidence and self-esteem, to a young woman who found her own way, but at the same time was being told that I thought I was better than others. Go figure! The truth of the matter was, they envied me. They wished that they had my drive and ambition, but because they lacked it, they put me down to make themselves feel better.

Never allow anyone to project their fears, insecurities, negative thoughts, and behaviors onto you. Honestly, they wish they were like you and had the courage to step out on faith and accomplish half the things of which you are capable. But because they lack ambition, they will try to dim your light. Don't let anyone tell you what you can or cannot do, no matter what. That's for you to decide. Always remember that you can do hard things. So go for it. Everything you desire is worth striving for. And if you fail, learn from your mistakes, re-strategize, then try again.

Also, re-evaluate your inner circle and find genuine people who will truly love you, support you, tell you the truth in love, and will be your biggest cheerleader. Seek those who will not criticize you simply because they don't understand God's vision for your life. Don't expect for everyone to understand or agree with your life's vision and purpose, so stop allowing others to block what God has already orchestrated and ordained for you.

I thank God for my mother. She has been and still is my biggest cheerleader and supporter. Even when my husband or those in my inner circle did not see the vision for my life, she said and still says to me, "Don't quit. Keep going. It doesn't matter when "they" get there. Just stay the course and keep going and when "they" look up, you'll be at the finish line too." I've always taken what she said to me to heart and her statements have been the driving force in my life. In high school and in the earlier years of my life, I would often compare myself to other family members and friends. I could not understand why my mother, sisters, and I were always the ones in the groups who endured and struggled the most. There was a moment that I wondered if God even loved us because we were the ones to always have it the hardest. Not only did I come to realize that God loved us, but all that we endured made us strong, resilient, and independent young women.

We've had to work twice, sometimes three times as hard to persevere and what didn't kill us just made us stronger. What would have taken some out and caused them to fail, I used as fuel to keep going and pushing through. When reflecting on that moment, I couldn't help but to think of the acronym P.U.S.H. (Push Until Something Happens), (Pray Until Something Happens), or (Persevere Until Something Happens). Through PUSHing, I have launched several businesses, graduated from college, became a Certified Life and Business Coach, launched my own television show and podcast, won Mrs. South Carolina Plus

America 2023, and last but not least, I yielded to the calling on my life to become an ordained Minister.

Thriving by God's Grace...

Life has lead me down many paths. Even though I was involved in extracurricular activities in high school, I led a sheltered life. I was not permitted to go out a lot and I can count the number of school dances I attended on one hand. I had one boyfriend at the time who I was allowed to date, but we rarely went out, so I didn't get much exposure while growing up.

After leaving my small home town to attend college, I continued to struggle with fitting in. I felt like I didn't belong; not because I could not do the work, but because it was more of a culture shock. I envied some of the other students because they seemed like they were built for campus life. They adjusted to college much better than I did and most seemed happy to be there. I know that I would've done better had I taken the first year off post high school but as the saying goes, hind sight is 20/20.

Although I was excited to attend college, I was tired mentally and physically. However, I was determined to make it because I did not want to return home. I hated it there. I felt the same way in high school and that is the reason why I was involved in multiple extracurricular activities in addition to working part-time. There is a saying that everything happens for a reason. I was able to get through my first year and a half of college before taking a semester off. That semester turned into almost 10 years before I was able to return to school to earn an Associate of Applied Science in Physical Therapist Assistant degree. However, it was during my first 18 months where I learned more about myself and is also when I met my husband.

It wasn't until I got married that I was battle tested and had to exercise that innate strength, fierceness and focus that I discovered earlier in my young adult life. I knew I was strong, but I did not know how strong I was until after the I do's. I got married at the early age of 21. When I met the love of my life, I learned early in our relationship that he had been recently diagnosed with epilepsy, a neurological disorder that causes seizures. As a 19-year-old young woman, I did not know exactly what it all meant and how it would impact our relationship. All I knew was that I had fallen in love with him and that I was going to see him through this ordeal.

We dated for almost three years before marrying. Because you never know what others are going through, you should always show kindness and love regardless. On my wedding day one of my closest family members told me that my marriage was not going to last. Imagine how that made me feel. I literally went from feeling euphoric to how I used to feel in the past when I wasn't sure of myself. She made me feel as if I didn't deserve to be happy on what should have been one of the most special days of my life. Although her comment bothered me for a while, but then I realized that what she said came from a place of pain and resentment. She was not married, had four children, and was not in a relationship with any of the fathers who impregnated her; yet I was the one whose marriage was not going to last. I was "crack" in her eyes, so for me to find someone who loved me was not supposed to be my reality.

In that moment, she was probably wondering how and why this was happening for me. And the fact that my husband and I looked happy didn't help either. Little did she know we were dealing with my pregnancy and my husband's newly diagnosed disorder all while trying to begin our new life together as one. There were countless doctor's appointments, new medicines, and eventually deciding to opt for brain surgery to control his seizures.

During this ordeal, we also had numerous vehicles repossessed and lost our home. Because his condition was so up and down, I knew that I had to go back to school to earn a degree to pursue a career that would sustain our family in the event that I was going to be the sole provider. Right before my clinicals to become a Licensed Physical Therapist Assistant, we had to relinquish our home. We packed our belongings, put them in storage, and with our two small children, we moved what was left into a hotel for three months until we could find more affordable housing. Thankfully, we were blessed with in-laws who were willing to help us out during our time of need.

Being homeless, a caregiver of an independent spouse, a full-time employee and student, and raising a young family was more than enough to break me. But somehow, I was able to tap into strength I didn't realize I had, and guess what, we persevered and made it through. Even with all of that, life still was not easy afterwards. However, what it all taught me was that if we were able to make it through what we endured, then there was nothing we could not withstand. Yes, life was hard and at times, it still is. But I believe that God did not bring me to these moments if He did not intend to bring me through them.

Being imperfectly fierce and focused is not about being perfect. In fact, it is the complete opposite. When you break down the word imperfect, it says "I'm perfect." When I think about being imperfectly fierce and focused, I'm reminded of all of the things that makes a person imperfect and then drawing strength and resilience from them. Growing up in poverty, being homeless, losing my vehicles, being exposed to domestic violence, and suspending my college career could have literally destroyed me. But instead, I picked myself up, dusted myself off, and got back into the fight. That is what life is about; taking those moments that are designed to destroy you and making living examples out of them. It's about being bold with your ambitions, confident in your decisions, understanding your worth, recognizing your resiliency, appreciating your tenacity, and walking in your truth. That is what makes you imperfectly fierce and focused.

My favorite scripture is Proverbs 3:6, "In all thy ways acknowledge Him and He will direct thy paths." Failure is not an option when you keep God first in everything you do, acknowledge your wins, and learn from your losses. If you continue to do this, you will create a life that reflects an imperfectly fierce and focused mindset and witness firsthand the desires of your heart come to pass.

Biography

Rev. Keever Lernise Murdaugh is an Executive Business, Automation and Media Specialist, and Leadership Development Coach from Camden, South Carolina. She helps leaders implement soft skills training and workshops and teaches them how to effectively introduce automated systems to improve profit margins, time management, and decrease stress levels.

In addition, she teaches her clients how to leverage their digital footprint to improve their credibility while maximizing their exposure and visibility. She's an entrepreneur and small business owner, a licensed physical therapy assistant, an international motivational speaker, a certified life and business coach, an ordained minister, an advocate and board member and a TV, podcast host, and producer of the #1 TV show and podcast "Keever's Place." This year she had the distinct privilege of being crowned Mrs. South Carolina Plus America.

Her favorite scripture is Proverbs 3:6, "In all thy ways acknowledge Him and He will direct thy path." Connect with Keever @ Linktr.ee/KeeverMurdaugh and subscribe to her TV Show and Podcast on all digital platforms, Facebook, Instagram and YouTube @KeeversPlace.

"It is not the critic who counts; not the man who points out how the strong man stumbles, or where the doer of deeds could have done them better. The credit belongs to the man who is actually in the arena, whose face is marred by dust and sweat and blood; who strives valiantly; who errs, who comes short again and again, because there is no effort without error and shortcoming; but who does actually strive to do the deeds; who knows great enthusiasms, the great devotions; who spends himself in a worthy cause; who at the best knows in the end the triumph of high achievement, and who at the worst, if he fails, at least fails while daring greatly, so that his place shall never be with those cold and timid souls who neither know victory nor defeat."

~Theodore Roosevelt

My Zig-Zag Journey
Amie Arizmendi

Like everyone else, I was born into this big wide world without instructions. I like instructions, but there seemed to be none. My parents were doing the best they could although I didn't know that then. There was so much I wanted to understand. I watched the world go by, taking it all in while deciding what it all meant based on my life's experiences and knowledge.

We look for order naturally and try to make sense of the world so that we can learn how to operate within its social standards. It took me a long time to realize that many of our social norms were made up. However, one thing that amazed me was when I learned that we were consumers. While that is a fact, we are also creators. We have an inherent right to create the life we want. I didn't realize this growing up. I was told, "Children are to be seen and not heard." I tended toward being a rule follower so when I was given this rule I followed it. I wasn't showing up in the world as who I was meant to be because I was living a suppressed life. I noticed everything and drew my own conclusions, mostly. Somewhere along the way I decided I did not want to be a burden to my overworked and underpaid mother. So, guess what ... I wasn't a burden. I faded into the background. I lived most of my life unseen and unheard. I was mad that my mom allowed me to grow up like that until I took responsibility for the decision I had made.

I wonder what life would have looked like for me if I had chosen differently. Instead of focusing on what I didn't want I could have just as easily decided to create what I wanted. The thing is, back then I didn't have a clue. The old adage, "if I knew then what I know now I would have chosen differently" resounds loudly like clanging symbols at the end of a great orchestra performance. Hindsight is 20/20 and offers opportunities for growth and change for those willing to embrace it.

Many people resist change. Rhetorically speaking, why is that?

My mom barely made it to the hospital when it was my time to be born. That's another story for another time, so I will spare the details. The point is, I was ready to enter the world before the world was ready to receive me. That said, in many ways I have felt ahead of my time. I struggled in school just so I would feel like I belonged. It also didn't help that we moved during my sixth-grade year. Instantly, I had to leave the place where I was familiar and was left to figure out how to make new friends to fit in. However, I don't think I ever really did. And if I did, I certainly told myself I didn't.

For most of my life, I have felt that way. I was an old soul. However, being viewed that way can be beneficial and challenging. One benefit is accepting, perhaps, more easily that you don't fit in. When you notice it, it doesn't seem to matter as much because you realize there is more to behold in this great world.

I knew I was not created to fit in, although I wanted to so badly. I wanted to be liked and feel included. Many of us have the same desire. But because some of us fear missing out, it is why our focus is on what others are doing. I thought if I made everyone's life easier they would like me.

They didn't. Nevertheless, I tried my best to be what others needed until one day I decided that it was time to live for me. Not everyone likes it when you decide to do so and that is ok. No one else can live my life. So I have a firm rule that I will do whatever I want to do with my life as long as I am not harming others in the process.

Growing up I also had a scarcity mentality. I saw my parents struggle and assumed that's the way it had to be. I lived my life from paycheck to paycheck. There were so many self-sabotaging behaviors that created this scenario. I didn't learn until later in life the value of choice. I have been making choices all my life but didn't quite understand just how valuable they were. Until one day, many years into adulthood, I lifted my head out of the sand and realized I had created the life I was living. Life can be filled with scarcity, but it can also be filled with abundance. That is the life to which we all are called.

You get to choose the way your life plays out. I get it, some of you may be saying, "yeah, but when I was a child my parents had the say so." While you are right, you still get to choose what to retain from your upbringing and the things that no longer serve you. Have you decided to slide into the ever-comfy status quo, or will you go against the grain and create the life you want?

As a child, I never really understood the number of choices I was making . I can't say what would have been different back then because it's really a losing game compared to what I think I may have missed out on. I am where I am today, and I am grateful that I know what I know now and that I can share it with others.

I perceived my older sister was my grandma's favorite. My younger sister is my adoptive dad's only biological child. In my young mind, I created a story that left me lost in the middle. I did not know where I belonged or how my life mattered from a young age throughout the first half of my life. My biological dad was gone by the time I was 2 years old. The struggles that he and mom had were too much, so they decided to end their marriage. Many of their decisions impacted me; but the one that hit me the most was refusing to come around if he could not bring gifts to my sisters and me. So, I grew up with lots of questions. Who am I? Why do I like this and not that? What is it about my health that I don't I know? What might my life have looked like had my biological dad been more present? Although my adoptive dad was a great, I did not realize it fully as a child growing up. He provided a roof over our heads, made sure we had clothes to wear and food to eat. However, I wanted more than the basics. My longing for more was left unmet. This caused ripple effects in my life that manifested much later. Namely, insecurities, feeling unseen and unheard, and not using my voice to speak up for myself.

As I mentioned earlier, I was the girl who was taught that children are to be seen and not heard. So that's what I did because I was a rule follower. I wanted to be approved of and avoid disappointing others. As a result, I observed life throughout my life. I was especially good at observing others. I noticed their faces, especially their eyes, whether or not they smiled or frowned, even their eyebrows. I noticed how people fidgeted or if they were too stoic. I noticed it all. People and their mannerisms fascinate me.

Through observation and some training, I honed the skill of noticing unspoken nuances. For example, I notice when a person's face changes color, the annoying habit of how they touch their face when uncomfortable topics of conversation are being discussed, or when they twist or run their fingers through their hair.

Creating stories. One time in college English class I had to write a short story about noticing others in prose. That assignment was right up my alley and I nailed it. I went to the local Denny's and sat in a booth across the room from a family having dinner. As I sat down, I scanned the room to see what stood out to me the most. However, I kept coming back to this one family, so they became the subject of my paper. The family included a mom, dad, and their older son who appeared to be high school age. Although they seemed to have an element of fun among them, I also noticed when they became silent. I created a whole story around what they most likely enjoyed doing in life and how they made a living. While I do not like to create stories about others this is what I was tasked to do. As it is with this task, I realize we all create stories in our lives based on our experiences.

Everyone has a right to share their story and I'm here for all of it. It is through other's stories we can connect, learn and grow. This is a daring objective however because society teaches us not to connect deeply. Unfortunately, this has gotten worse throughout my lifetime. We are more disconnected from others now than I have ever experienced before. We desperately need connection. What about you? Are you connected with others who support and lift you up? Or do you remain attached to the fray?

Family secrets can be devastating. I was touched inappropriately. I kept this secret throughout my childhood and most of my adult years. I did not dare tell anyone. What if no one believed me? What if they blamed me? Sadly, I did not feel I had a support structure that I could trust with my secret. So I suffered in silence; allowing the trauma to dig deep into my psyche. I betrayed myself by keeping the secret hidden. It caused me to have broken relationships with family; to be misunderstood; to be blamed for trying to stay afloat while I navigated life harmed. However, the bigger issue was not being able to ask for help. I was making grown-up choices while in elementary school. I wasn't an anomaly; this type of thing happens to many others. Academically I did well but was not so great at fitting in to any circle. It took me years to accept that I wasn't meant to. However, I now know that I am meant to fit everywhere, not in one circle here and there.

I was in a car accident and sustained head trauma. After completing rehabilitation, I moved to a new school on the other side of the state. Boyfriends came and went yet some only wanted what my body could offer them. However, I did have one long-term relationship while in high school. But after graduation we went our separate ways because of what I wanted to do in life. When I shared with my boyfriend and his family that I wanted to be an airline attendant, they thought that it was a crazy idea. Sadly, I let their opinions impact me to some degree. Since they were not in support of my goals, I concluded that maybe they were not the family for me. Despite breaking up at one point, we got back together given that he was someone with whom I was familiar and felt safe. My relationship with him was comfortable, the land of familiarity. We eventually ended our relationship, for good.

Wanting more out of life, I decided to join the Navy. I had no idea what I was getting into, yet I knew I wanted to see who I could become. I stepped into the unknown to make a path and find my way. The military was a mixed bag. There were great experiences as well as heart-wrenching ones. However, I am grateful for all the places I traveled to and the things I was able to see. One of the biggest lessons I learned was that people are people. Although our skin color and cultures may vary, at the end of the day we all have the option to choose which way we will go, at least in the United States.

Although I came from meager means, I am determined to create something big that looks vastly different from my origins. I am here for it. I am blessed to have an innate desire to see what I am capable of despite my circumstances. What about you? Have you given up or decided to settle for mediocrity? I am curious about what your choice will be.

I enrolled in college and took a few accounting courses. But unfortunately, I ran out of money living on my own. I was running from my past while trying to hold onto it ever so tightly at the same time. Who would I be without it? There was so much I repressed, and I didn't even know how to let it go.

While stationed in Pensacola, Florida, for training, I met an amazing man, fell in love, got engaged, ended the engagement, but I also began to come to terms with the skeletons I stuffed in my closet. All the things I endured throughout life that could have easily broken me came to the surface, one by one. But I stuffed it all back down to keep it hidden. I was not ready to deal with it all.

While at my first duty station, I was eager to integrate and learn all there was to learn about my new job and the ship I was assigned to. This is also where I met my future husband. We were engaged for only a short time when I learned that his 7-year-old son would be coming to live with us due to some unfortunate circumstances he was facing. We were so broken, carrying all of our baggage from the past with us; nevertheless, we tied the knot. I felt as though I married him for his son's sake. I lived to make everyone else's life better, remember? I neglected myself – a pattern I didn't identify and accept until years later. This was a habit that did not serve me, and I did not know exactly how to change it.

Full disclosure ... I entered into the marriage naively. Although I loved my fiancé, I was too young to get married. Being thrown into the responsibility of motherhood, I immediately felt that our relationship had gone from being playful and fun to being super serious. I felt trapped. I told him that I wasn't going to marry him for the convenience of creating a happy home. However, we discussed it, and he reassured me that we would be okay, so I decided to marry him anyway. Yet again, I rescinded my fears somewhat and put myself on the backburner to please others.

I began to awaken to the habits that were keeping me from achieving my best. Although my heart was in a well-meaning place, my mind knew that I was stuck in a broken cycle of personal despair. I watched my mom endlessly give herself to others, especially her family. While admirable, this way of living often leads to dead ends because people will come and go and keep taking and taking. I didn't realize until later that I had formed a pattern of pleasing people.

So here I was married and a new mom to a bonus son who had been abused and neglected. This changed me in ways unimaginable. I did my best to help this young boy learn to accept life and let go of what was not helpful to him. I didn't know then what I know now. I couldn't help him as much as I wanted to, but I was able to connect him with resources I thought would benefit him the most. He attended a behavioral health center only to pick up other undesirable behaviors.

I learned he had a honeymoon pattern. He would go into the center and come out shortly thereafter because he had a keen survival mechanism and would learn the system. He'd be home for roughly 10 days, and things were better, but then suddenly he'd revert back to his old ways. This was my first glimpse into seeing how broken our healthcare system was and in many ways, still is. While I am thankful for it on the one hand I also believe that we can do better. One of the realizations was the pharmaceutical regimen my bonus son was put on. While the meds helped some they were not the answer. And I was unwilling to keep giving them to him as a temporary fix that could possibly cause long term health effects. I was losing myself in the fight for his life and freedom. I was not successful as a full-time employee and a full-time single parent (my husband deployed throughout our marriage) to my bonus son. This was my first instance of realizing how little control I had over a life beyond my own. He moved back and forth between our home and his mom's. The second lesson that I didn't quite fully realize until about 20 years later was that this situation was less than ideal for him. Admittedly so, I couldn't do it all. I tried yet found myself lacking some things. This period of time was pivotal for me as I began to understand why I was placed on this Earth.

So, where are you sacrificing yourself endlessly for others and possibly not even being recognized for your contribution? How is it beneficial for you? How is it helping you to be, do and have all for which you are hoping?

I was pregnant with my first baby, a girl. Five weeks into the pregnancy, I vomited on my way to work. Not sure what to make of it, I contacted the doctor. I was told to keep an eye on it as this can be normal. My husband and I went to a murder mystery theater, and I started bleeding. The visit to the emergency room confirmed there was something abnormal about the pregnancy. I was instructed to follow up with my obstetrician who advised me to have an Amniocentesis done to make sure there were no other issues with my developing baby. I researched the procedure and had read enough. "No, I said!" I refused to jeopardize my baby. At that moment I decided to advocate for her and do what I believed was best. I was told by the medical professionals that some parents decide to abort the baby after having an amniocentesis done. However, that was not an option for me. I told them they did not have the liberty to discuss terminating the pregnancy with me anymore. I could not believe their nonchalant approach to life, although I knew I lived in a world where this was commonplace for some. That was none of my business and again, it was not an option for me, period.

I delivered a healthy baby overall. However, she had to have three surgeries before she was 18 months old. I learned just how adaptable and innovative I could be. I loved my baby girl. She was perfect. But on the other hand my marriage was not ... another story for another time.

I was trying so hard to prove myself in this world. Years ago when I was struggling the most with self-love, I heard recording artist Colbie Caillat's song, "Try." The lyrics truly resonated with me. Throughout the song Caillat sings about how we don't have to try so hard to fit in and prove who we are. I realized this during the second half of my life. Little by little I began to emerge from the safe cocoon I had been living in.

Psalm 139 reminds me that I am fearfully and wonderfully made. I am an original and have no need to compare myself to others. This was something that took me years to learn and embrace. What about you? How are you showing up as your best self, day in and day out? Are you allowing yourself to have good days or days that you wouldn't write home about? What thoughts are helping you overcome the past that may be riddled with doubt and fear? Are you truly living, or just existing? As you ponder these questions, don't dwell on your imperfections. Always remember that you have the ability to fiercely focus on the goals and desires that God has placed on the inside of you. When you know who and whose you are, EVERYTHING CHANGES!

Biography

Ms. Amie Arizmendi is the Founder of ABR Coaching, Consulting & Training. She is a Yaeger-trained certified speaker, author, and consultant who also spent 20 years in the U.S. Navy where she worked as a researcher and advocate for suicide prevention, equal opportunity, and helping victims of sexual assault.

Today, she serves as a Leadership and Life Coach, who excels in transforming corporations, churches, teams, as well as individual clients. Through these partnerships, she helps them to successfully identify and move past their limitations, so they are able to embrace and live their greatest life yet!

ABR Coaching, Consulting & Training strives to inspire others, assist organizations increase productivity and engagement, and optimize the whole person.

Ms. Arizmendi is a Licensed Clinical Mental Health Counselor and an expert in neuroscience and behavior with certificates in Hypnotherapy, Quantum Time Techniques, Public Speaking, Ho'oponopono, Reiki (Level 1), as well as a Master Practitioner of Neuro-Linguistic Programming.

> "Don't not judge me by my successes, judge me by how many times I fell down and got back up again."
>
> ~Nelson Mandela

Confidence Trumps Perfectionism Every Time

Jacqueline Kaba-Harrison

There was a time when I believed that I didn't have a story to tell. I felt as if I had nothing of value to share, much less something meaningful that would help other women. Honestly speaking, if I didn't value myself as a person what value would I have to offer others? For many years, a dark cloud hovered over me and all I heard was blaring messages of self-doubt, unworthiness, and incapability. This left me feeling defeated, powerless, and voiceless.

Fast forward to 2023, the feelings from my past no longer haunt me and now I know without a shadow of a doubt that I am capable, competent, valuable and worthy of abundance. I'm excited about what the future holds.

For as long as I can remember I have always been a daddy's girl. I am the eldest of three children and the only girl. I recall sitting beside my dad and we would talk. He would tell me stories and I would ask millions of questions. My father was like God to me, and I was his little girl. I could talk to him about anything and would tell him when I was worried about something or if something was bothering me. He would just listen and near the end of the conversation would reassure me that everything was going to be alright and would work themselves out. So that's what I became accustomed to. I saw my father as a mentor, a teacher and someone to whom I looked up. He was someone I could always depend on; someone I could trust and who always had my best interest at heart. Looking back in retrospect it seems hard to believe. Children naturally love their parents without judgement, and I was no different.

In my eyes, my father could do or say no wrong. He instilled many beliefs in me. I remember very vividly him saying things like, "I can't stand a liar and if you lie then you will steal." He also stressed the importance of having good moral character and keeping your word. He believed if you said you were going to do something then do it. I looked up to my father. He was the perfect example of a quality person although in reality, he was flawed just like everyone else. In my eyes, my father was a good person and parented my sisters and me the best way he knew how. When you're young you never really think about how your parents were raised or whether or not they had a happy childhood. It's only when we become an adult that we begin to think about these things. As a social worker I know that people are strongly influenced by their environment. For example, I don't remember my father ever telling me that he loved me or that he was proud of me, unless he had been drinking. However, I later learned as an adult that his mother never told him that she loved him. That said, oftentimes people just continue the cycle. They emulate their parents and believe that because they turned out okay then so will their children.

"You are not that smart." "You will have to work twice as hard as everyone else to achieve the same thing." I remember my father saying those words to me like it was yesterday! I sometimes get teary eyed when thinking about it.

I was born and raised in Detroit and attended public school until I was 12 years old. They were primarily all black, but what I remember most is how much I liked my teachers and fellow students. However, when we relocated to Southfield, Michigan that all changed. During that time Southfield was majority White so that was a huge change for me. I don't remember talking with my parents about how I felt, and as far as I know they believed everything was fine. Prior to moving, I had always received pretty good grades in school, but that changed as well. I'm not sure why exactly. I don't know if it were because the work was more difficult, or that I struggled with the transition to middle school, or that my self-confidence was low, and I didn't believe I could succeed. Whatever the reason, I was getting C's and D's and wasn't doing well at all. However, I felt as if I had something to prove to my teachers, my parents, and myself. But most of all, the one person who I wanted to please the most was my father. I wanted him to believe that I could turn my grades around. I remember feeling so frustrated at times while doing my homework because I didn't understand the work; and this continued throughout high school.

Getting poor grades definitely didn't help my self-confidence. My father tried to help me and said things like, "Jack (that's what he called me), you're not that smart, but in order to do better, you are going to have to work twice as hard as everyone else." "I know it's not fair, but that's just the way it is sometimes; life is not fair." Honestly, at the time I don't remember how his comments made me feel exactly. One might think it made me feel bad, but in all actuality, I was used to hearing comments like that and over time, I began accepting it as truth. In looking back, it's a possibility that it was my father's way to motivate me. Or just maybe, it made me even more determined to learn the work so when I got a good grade, it made me feel good to show it to my father and seem him crack a smile. He would say, "Wow, you actually did it, but next time I want you to do better." Again, I don't recall exactly how it made me feel, but I know it didn't make me angry. No matter what, I still looked up to him and still believed that everything he did and said was right. I idolized him. I remember one of my friends saying to me, "Wow, you really look up to your father," and in my mind I thought, doesn't everyone look up to their dad? Although I worked really hard, at best, my grades were average throughout high school. There were times when I would bring home a B and my father would say, "Okay, but next time make it an A."

I rarely received any praise for a job well done. I was told not to celebrate a win until I achieved my goal completely. It was frowned upon to celebrate any progress along the way. I'm not sure why, but to him it seemed as if the small wins were insignificant. Even after I reached my goal, instead of celebrating my wins he expected me to start working on the next goal. This thought process stayed with me for many years.

I would ask my father for advice on just about everything (except boys). He was ever so happy and willing to give it, however as I got older the more problematic it became. As a result, I decided to start making my own decisions without consulting him and he wasn't happy about that at all. So I became fearful and doubted my ability to make decisions on my own and believed that I needed to consult others for their opinion.

When looking back at what was happening at home as well as at school, it was these events that caused me to develop an inferiority complex and would shape me and have an impact on my life that I never imagined.

I wanted to be popular in school so badly and would fantasize different scenarios where my classmates would see me as smart, pretty, and likable. However, in reality, my situation was quite the opposite. I was picked on and made fun of not because of my grades but because I was Black and quiet. When I was in the sixth grade, there was a young girl who befriended me, and we became best friends and remained best friends for more than 30 years. We had a favorite restaurant that we would go to and sit for several hours sipping coffee and eating slices of French silk pie. It was during those times that many of my life's decisions were made. I would draft up a list of pros and cons (in my head) and present it to her and without fail, we talked through it, and she would help me to decide what or what not to do. To think there was a time I had so much self-doubt that I believed someone else knew more about what was good for me that I did for myself is scary. It became a pattern of convenience and the more I did it, the more dependent I became on others. If it weren't my best friend then it would have been whoever was close to me at that time. It could be something as simple as buying clothes, selecting hairstyles, or the best place to buy groceries. I didn't even trust my own judgement about what style of clothing looked good on me. For so long I entrusted all of my major decisions to my father and others so much so that I had no say so over my life.

As a young adult, the feelings of not being smart enough and incapable of making sound decisions were always hanging over my head. I never discussed them openly with anyone. It was my own little secret. I constantly limited myself by placing myself inside of a box. There was no one to blame but me. I felt like an imposter and feared that at any minute my secret might be revealed.

Throughout undergraduate school I continued to feel less than, and that I would never catch up to everyone else's level. I remember saying to myself on the first day of class, "You are going to need extra help if you expect to pass this class." Even when I participated in study groups I felt apprehensive about participating because I was nervous about not holding up my end of the bargain. I was afraid that others would soon find out my secret, that I was dumb. Deep down inside I felt inadequate, that I didn't have the necessary skills to succeed, and I didn't want anyone to find out. Every time I started a new class the same feelings of insecurity would come rushing in. In the end and to my surprise, I got pretty good grades. I attributed my success to being proactive with studying, asking questions during class, and participating in study groups. When I made mistakes on a project, I would ruminate over it and consider it a failure. This type of behavior was extremely draining, provoked anxiety, and contributed to negative thoughts about myself. As a result, it spilled over into all areas of my life -- employment, personal and professional relationships, and of course, making crucial decisions.

I wore myself out to a point where I became a perfectionist. Everything had to be just so. At the time I had a word processor, and I remember stressing over not getting the paper straight in the machine. I had been up half the night finishing my paper but could not get the damn paper straight in the word processor. In and out, in and out, it was like I just couldn't stop myself. If anything was slightly off such as a footnote not being formatted correctly, paragraph spacing that was wasn't perfect, a space missing after a period, or a slight smudge of ink on the paper was cause for a reprint. This type of obsessive behavior became common place for me.

When I graduated from college with my undergraduate degree I was so excited! I had actually forgotten about this until now. After graduation, I remember talking with my father and desperately wanting him to tell me how proud he was of me for receiving my degree. Although he said that he was proud of me, he negated it by insinuating that I had someone else complete my assignments and take my tests for me in order to graduate. He seemed to think it was funny. I just gave him a look and shook my head in disbelief. To be honest at the time I wasn't angry or offended, given that I had become accustomed to his ways and didn't think much of it. But now looking back on that moment makes me livid and sad at the same time. I have an 11-year-old son and I cannot imagine saying anything like that to him. I will do everything that's in me to uplift and make him believe in himself. He will know that he's smart, talented, gifted and can achieve whatever he puts his mind to. I never want him to feel less than, undeserving, or to limit himself.

I would watch others from a far and cheer them on, never once thinking about using my gifts or skills. In fact, I didn't feel as if my talents or skills measured up to my peers. I limited myself to my dreams which also limited my reality. The best way to describe it is, I always felt like I was on the outside looking in. Like most children, I also wanted to know what it felt like to be loved, accepted, happy, and worthy of success. But sadly, I never believed that I would ever experience those feelings. I felt as if there was an invisible fence that I was not allowed to cross.

Although I was extremely proud of myself for obtaining my undergraduate degree, I didn't believe I had adequate experience compared to my fellow graduates. So when it was time to search for a job I would send out as many resumes as possible, including applying for jobs in which I wasn't interested. And as chance would have it, it was those employers who I usually heard back from and felt compelled to accept the job offer because I didn't believe I would get any better ones. So, I decided to settle.

However, over time a shift occurred, and I began looking at myself differently in a positive way. Today, I can honestly say that I believe in myself and my ability to manifest whatever I desire. I know that I know that I am worthy of abundance and possess the necessary skills to achieve whatever I put my mind to. Believing in yourself and feeling worthy go hand in hand. They are both necessary to achieve one's personal and professional goals. However, if a person feels worthy of abundance but looks outside of themselves for the answers, then they won't be successful. In the same light, if one feels that they have the answers within, yet they don't feel worthy they won't be successful either.

The person I was in the past no longer exists. Those feelings of inadequacy and placing limitations on myself are OVER. I now know that the sky is the limit, and it feels invigorating to be a co-creator along this journey called life. I am finally free of that dark cloud that hovered over my head telling me what I could and couldn't do. Of course this transformation did not happen overnight and there was no fairy Godmother who made my wishes come true. This process began when I was about 23 or 24 years old, and it has been ongoing. I had several tools that I used in my arsenal that helped to turn my life around. While everything doesn't work for everybody, I had to find what worked for me that would help me achieve my long-term goals.

I've experienced firsthand what it feels like to lack self-confidence and suffer from low self-esteem and how it negatively impacts every aspect of your life. If left unchecked, they will permeate your life like cancer, causing you to make poor decisions, as well as limit yourself to what's possible. If I can prevent one person from experienced what I went through, then I'll know that my labor is not in vain. That said, I have created a workbook that focuses on how to overcome negative self-talk and self-sabotaging behaviors that prevents a person from showing up boldly, consistently and with intentionality in their business. Unfortunately, many people go through life without walking in their purpose or achieving their full potential. There are numerous reasons why that happens. However, one of the main reasons is because they have a limited mindset instead of a growth mindset, which causes them to believe that they can't. As a result, they doubt their ability to achieve their goals. Think about it, if you believed beyond a shadow of doubt that you would not fail at accomplishing your goals, would there be a reason not to do it. The answer is no. However, what usually causes a person to doubt their ability to achieve their goals is a lack of self-confidence. That's why it's critical for parents to start teaching their children early how to develop unshakeable confidence.

I decided to serve as one of the co-authors of *Imperfectly Fierce & Focused* because the title resonated with me, given that spent a large part of my life battling perfectionism! I measured my success on whether I completed a project perfectly or not. Achieving perfectionism was my way of convincing myself subconsciously that I was good enough, smart enough, and skilled enough. Over the years I wore myself out while completing homework trying to ensure I received the highest grade possible. I viewed my flaws as shameful, unacceptable and damaging to my character, resulting in me feeling unworthy and undeserving. However, I have learned to embrace my imperfections and flaws and understand that they make me unique and special. Showing up in the world authentically allows me to focus more on conquering my personal and professional goals and less on my flaws.

The following are several ways to develop unshakable self-confidence. These techniques can be applied at any time in your personal and professional life. First, pay close attention to who you surround yourself with. Never underestimate the importance of including likeminded individuals in your circle. As I shared earlier, I grew up in an extremely negative household where my father, who was the patriarch, controlled everything that went on. My father was the type of person that felt like his whole life was one bad situation after another. It became evident that he learned early on that it was best not to hope for much to avoid being disappointed in the event that things didn't work out. He passed this way of thinking on to me, as a way to protect me from being hurt, I suspect. Also, my father didn't believe women were capable of greatness. He would say things like, "This world is only going to let you get so far before it knocks you back down." Or "You wouldn't have any luck at all if it wasn't for bad luck." What I have learned is if you surround yourself with individuals who don't believe in themselves, then it is very likely that they won't believe in and/or support you in your journey. I noticed a significant shift in my life and business when I sought out individuals who believed in themselves and were walking in their purpose. When you surround yourself with individuals who believe they can create the lifestyle they truly desire and deserve, then you can support and encourage each another and exchange resources.

A second way to develop unshakeable self-confidence is to celebrate your wins, no matter how big or small. Oftentimes we become so focused on the end goal that we forget to celebrate our progress along the way. Celebrating your progress keeps you motivated to continue while helping to boost your confidence. When you believe in you ... most likely other will too. I was taught not to celebrate my small wins, but to keep going until I achieved my goal. Even then celebrations were not allowed so I could focus on the next one. There were no pats on the back given or any other accolades for that matter. A third way to create unshakeable self-confidence is by venturing outside of your comfort zone. This is simply doing things that you have never done before. When you take on new projects and complete them, your confidence level shoots through the roof and you're able to handle whatever comes your way. When you get used to operating outside of your comfort zone, not only will your confidence soar, but you will also adopt a fearless attitude because you now know that you can do hard things. For example, I was able to create unshakeable self-confidence after taking a West African dance class. When I was 10 years old, I took ballet, tap, and modern dance. However, when I was introduced to West African dance in my mid 20's it was like nothing I had ever experienced before. The music and movements were completely foreign to me. I had never heard African drum music before, much less danced to it. I also had never seen any African dance movements much less tried to learn them. Keep in mind there are numerous drum rhythms that are done by certain ethnic groups for specific purposes. So I was COMPLETELY outside of my comfort zone. There were many times I felt silly and defeated in class. I felt perfectly imperfect and thought I would never learn the dance moves, but I remained consistent and continued going to class. The more I went, the better I got. As time went on, I began to trust my ability to retain the dance moves and the rest is history.

The bottom line is this, whether it's life in general, owning a business, or learning something new; in order to grow, you must be willing to be uncomfortable. Perfection is not necessary, only progress is. Just resolve to be fierce and focused and trust the process. But above all, never give up! Your goals are waiting to be crushed on the other side.

Biography

Jacqueline Kaba-Harrison is a Confidence and Success Coach as well as the CEO of Realizing Your Potential, LLC, an organization specializing in empowering and inspiring African American women globally. Specifically, she helps entrepreneurs create effective strategies to eliminate negative self-talk and self-sabotaging behaviors that prevent them from taking their business to the next level.

Additionally, she provides them with a virtual platform to receive personal, professional and leadership development to help them scale their business. She is the Executive Producer of A

Queen's Round Table channel on the Women Win TV Network, the fastest growing all-woman TV Network, as well as the host of A Queen's Round Table Leadership Symposium, TV Show and Podcast.

Ms. Kaba-Harrison is also the visionary of *Born To Lead: Awakening The Leader Within* and *Women of Color United, My Health Is My Wealth: The Ultimate Guide for Practicing Self-care for Entrepreneurs* anthology book projects.

"And let us not grow weary while doing good, for in due season we shall reap if we do not lose heart."
~Galatians 6:9

"The process was not designed to be easy, but it is necessary for our growth. You can't go around it, run behind it, run beside it, nor go over it, you must go through it. It is during those pressured moments that refining is occurring. Trust the process. If you're patient, the end result will yield a diamond. Shine bright my Queens, YOU DESERVE IT."
~Fouchina Kirkendoll

Stay Out of the Trash
Fouchina Kirkendoll

Are you about to return to the same thing I delivered you from? One day when I was in the bathroom, that was the question God asked me ever so gently. For a brief moment, it shook me to my core because it reminded me of a period in my life when I thought I was going to lose my ever-loving mind. I allowed a man to dominate my thoughts and saturate my mind with toxicity that included doubt, lies, and manipulation. I didn't know whether I was coming or going, but I knew something had to change. I was serving two masters – God and my flesh and my flesh was winning on the battlefield of my mind. There is nothing more frustrating than knowing better and not doing better. I know I'm not the only one who's been guilty of that.

My first mistake was allowing who I thought was a "man of God" to deceive me. He knew the Word and could spit out chapter and verse like nobody's business. I was hooked immediately and gravitated to him unbeknownst of the secrets that existed beneath the surface.

Question to ponder: *How many of us have gotten so caught up in a relationship that we lost all common sense and were void of reality?*

It didn't matter what I "knew" the truth to be. I was more satisfied with what I "wanted" my truth to be, and I ran with it. Does this ring a bell? Or am I by myself? I saw a post on Facebook that read, "As people, we see in others what we want to see in them instead of seeing them for who they really are." Ouch!

How many times has God delivered us from something or someone, yet we find ourselves back where we started? Well that was me. There were times when I allowed myself to be toxic emotionally, physically, mentally, and spiritually. I was satisfied and believed that having a "piece of a man" was better than having no man at all. At the time, I didn't think I deserved better, so I settled for whoever. The interesting thing was sadly, I became comfortable in my own filth. Thank God for grace, right? I spent so many years in this toxic landfill that people did not understand why I downsized to a trash can, that protected me from the outside world, as well as limited space with one way in and one way out.

Emotionally speaking, while "living" in the trash can I allowed and accepted things that weren't good for me. Instead of rejecting his lies, betrayal, and disrespect I embraced them as precious mementos! PRAISE BREAK! When I think of the goodness of Jesus and all that He's done for me, my soul cries out Hallelujah! OK, back to the story!

Life in the trash can was one of the most disgusting, demeaning, and humiliating times of my existence on Earth, BUT GOD! Sadly, it was all I knew. I was content and felt comfortable and safe. However, there came a time in my life when l began observing how other women were attracting and marrying the men of their dreams, yet the same thing wasn't happening for me. So I began asking myself, "What does she have that I don't? I found myself comparing my looks to those who I believed to be less attractive than me and could not figure out for the life of me how they got who appeared to be "Mr. Right" and I was stuck with "Mr. Wrong." For years, I lived with resentment and envy.

It all began after my first and only marriage. It wasn't the best, BUT out of it I birthed a beautiful son and gained a better understanding of who I was and accepted many hard truths. There were also many lessons learned.

1. Never marry for sex.

2. Have an escape plan.

3. Never allow anyone to determine your worth.

4. Know who and whose you are at all times.

5. NEVER let go of God's unchanging hands.

Pearl of wisdom: *There's always a blessing in the messing.*

My marriage, separation, and divorce were so challenging and intense, that I was close to having a mental breakdown and wanting to commit suicide, BUT GOD! With Him I made it through! Although I was saved, I wasn't yet delivered from the trash can of life. I enjoyed the momentary victory of coming out of it, but I found myself slowly returning back to it. I was so used to being in unhealthy relationships that I didn't know what a healthy one looked like. I had no idea what it felt like for a man to treat me with dignity and respect. Honestly, I looked at it as a sign of weakness. So when I actually had a good man who treated me right, I had a hard time respecting him. Talk about being confused! Unfortunately, in the end I lost a good thing. Sadly, the relationships that followed were filled with more rejection and pain. I told myself, "You can take it girl; you should be used to it by now." But even in our filth, God is still watching, caring, loving, providing, and waiting for us to come back to Him.

Fast forward decades later, again I found myself in another unhealthy relationship. And again, there were more lessons learned:

Lesson 1. Never date a man who you're roommates with and whose name is not on the lease. I told myself, "If having sex is going to keep causing you to make dumb decisions, then you need to give it up completely." I came to the realization that it just wasn't worth it and decided to go cold turkey. That's when my season of abstinence began. My sex addiction was a result of being sexually abused as a child and it dictated too much of my life for far too long. Abstaining from sex was one of the hardest things I've ever done. Although it wasn't easy, it was necessary for my healing and growth. It was truly for my good, but more so for God's glory. I'd be lying if I said the struggle wasn't real. It still is, BUT I refuse to cave in to my temptations. With each victory God strengthens me and increases my faith in Him. Through praise and worship and reading the Word, I'm able to overcome sexual temptation. One thing I know for sure, is that God will provide a way of escape for any struggle that we face. The older I get, the better I get and I'm becoming stronger every day.

Lesson 2. There is nothing too hard for God … absolutely NOTHING. According to Pastor Mike McClure, "If it's HIS will, it's HIS bill!"

Our decisions always impact others and mine not only affected me, but they also affected my children. If I'm not careful they could also possibly affect my future grandchildren and generations to come. But I'm determined that this curse stops with me because if it doesn't … MY LEGACY is at stake! When I made the conscious decision to abstain from sex, I no longer walked around with "rose-colored" glasses on, and I was able to gain clarity.

Pearl of wisdom: *When you allow distractions to dominate your life, they cause you to be blinded by your reality. In other words you will see people and things how you want to see them instead of what or how they truly are.*

For once, it felt good to see and relate to people as people instead of using them for the temporary pleasures they had to offer. Food for thought, once the thrill is gone and reality sets in, you find yourself asking, "What in the ham and cheese sandwich was I doing?" Lord, thank you for saving a wretch like me!

Although sex is no longer an issue, I do miss it. However, every time an urge comes, I think back and remind myself of how far I've come. In no way do I want to give up eight years of purity for a moment of temporary pleasure that may not even be that good. After all that God has done in my life, the last thing that I want to do is to break my covenant with Him and lose His covering over my life, thus causing His grace to go bye-bye. Sometimes you have to ask yourself tough questions as you work your way through temptation. During one of those moments I had to say to myself, "Self, do you really want to start over again?" "Absolutely NOT!" "You know what, you're good!"

"NOT TODAY SATAN, NOT TODAY!" "I am picking up my cross and carrying it into the next phase of my life." I also had to get rid of other temptations (people, places, and things) that posed a threat to my journey. NEXT... STILL SAVED, BUT NOT YET DELIVERED FROM THE TRASH CAN. But keep rolling with me because we're going somewhere.

I had never been a huge fan of long-distance relationships; but ended up growing fond of them, so I thought. I had a dream about a childhood friend and decided to reach out to him through a family member. I left my phone number; he returned the call and left me a message, and we re-connected. When we finally spoke, I shared with him that he appeared in my dream, and I wanted to see how he was doing.

I said to myself, "OK China, you did your part, now it's time to move on." But no, I just couldn't stop there. I got caught up in the moment and what was meant for a reason became a season in my life. So instead of returning home, I stayed unpacked and settled down – what a BIG mistake. We started reminiscing about our childhood years and went down memory lane. I am a firm believer that a man's word is his bond. However, when I noticed the first lie he told, I dismissed it, and the next one and next. Then came the lack of attention and time. When I confronted him about his lies I was made to feel that I was wrong for calling him out on it, I digress! However, I started responding to him in a negative way, and with a harsh tone. After giving my life to Christ and becoming a new creation, I allowed him to take me out of my character and I returned to my old nature. Something was definitely wrong, but I loved him.

Word of caution: If you decide to embark on a long-distance relationship out of state, don't rush into it because time will reveal if there is someone else who also believes they are involved in a relationship with the same person. If this is truly a God-ordained relationship, more than likely you should not have to worry about exes interfering.

However, if you find yourself in a relationship like the one I was in, then I suggest having a hard conversation collectively and establishing a reasonable deadline to sever all ties.

Pearl of wisdom: When asking God for something, if it's His will, be ready to receive it and prepared to accept what HE shows you and believe Him the first time.

Although I asked God to reveal if I was the only woman in my friend's life multiple times, when He showed me that I wasn't, sadly, I still wanted to be with him (signs of familiarity). In my heart I truly wanted to believe I was the only one, but in reality I knew I wasn't.

Word of caution: *When making a video to send to someone, make sure that you're sending it to the right person, enough said.*

The final straw came when I received a video in error and listened to the recording. I must have watched and listened to that video at least 20 times to confirm that what I heard the first time was correct and clearly it was not meant for me. However, when I approached him about it, of course he lied to the point where we finally agreed to disagree. A few months went by, (yes, I said a few months) until I finally received an admission of truth. I just responded with "OK," but after thinking about what I said, I asked myself, "Are you really OK with saying OK?

I contacted my therapist, and he asked me if I was OK. I was a little taken back. I began thinking about what the characteristics of love were, and came to the realization that lies, manipulation, and deceit weren't among them. Not only was this relationship toxic, but it was also an unhealthy soul tie. I asked myself, "Is this God's will for your life?" I sought after God and told Him that I went instead of waiting to be sent. I told Him how sorry I was for causing this situation and that He was the only one who could break this soul tie.

Note: *A soul tie may form between a person, place, or thing and it doesn't have to be just physical.*

I asked God for a Word, and He delivered. I saw a sermon by a pastor at Rock City Church in Birmingham, Ala. who was discussing unhealthy soul ties. As he was going down the check list, they all pertained to me. I fell on my knees immediately and prayed to have it broken and to be healed. I began fasting ... no food, no water, and no outside communication, it was just me and God. Love does not involve lying, deceiving or manipulating others. God is love. While fasting, God also revealed my role in the situation. After the fast was over, I terminated the relationship.

However, during the process, I learned a few things:

1. You must be equally yoked.

2. Know the difference between a reason, a season, or a lifetime experience.

3. When you ask God for something, and He answers, obey and govern yourself accordingly.

Finally I was free, so I thought. I was at the lowest of lows and began missing him. I found myself looking for messages and pics, which by the way I deleted.

Word of caution: *Did you know that when you delete anything from your phone it stays in the trash can for 30 days?*

Well, I hit the jackpot and located all of his old messages and pictures. Then it hit me, and I said to myself, "CHINA, DO YOU REALIZE YOU'RE BACK IN THE TRASH! You've returned to the trash can ... OMG. You are actually rummaging through the trash like a bum." That shook me to my core and if that wasn't enough, God dropped 2 Peter 2:20-22 into my spirit. Paraphrasing, it says,

"You asked me to deliver you. I deliver you and you're going to go back to what you've been delivered from. You might as well not have even asked me. But it happened unto them according to the true proverb, the dog has returned to his own vomit!" Every time I thought about that scripture I cringed. That was it for me and I immediately cleared my trash can.

Pearl of wisdom: *Don't ever get so big to think that you delivered yourself from something or someone. If so, you may find yourself unprotected from God's covering and targeted by satan whose MO is to steal your peace, kill your destiny and destroy your life.*

Even after everything I endured, every now and again I still found myself going back to what was familiar! Sometimes in life you just have to walk away. Not only am I SAVED; I'm NOW DELIVERED! How many of you are going through the same or a similar situation where you find yourself living in and out of the trashcans of life? If that's you, I have some good news. You don't have to stay stuck in that situation; you have the ability to come out and stay out. The question is, "Are you tired of being sick and tired? If the answer is yes, it's GO TIME!

But how do I do that? I'm so glad you asked!

- Seek God first! Ask Him if the person or opportunity is HIS will for your life.

- Determine if you're ready to receive what you're asking God for; and if you're not, you've got some work to do.

- Pay attention and look for signs (seek God for the spirit of discernment).

- When signs are given, don't second guess them. Govern yourself accordingly and WALK AWAY.

- If you want something you've never had, you must do things you've never done!

- Trust God with all your heart and lean not to your own understanding. HE knows what's best for you even if you don't understand it. HE requires the faith of a mustard seed.

- Trust the process: you can't go around it; you must go through it.

The reason I hadn't attracted the one God has for me is because I was still smelling like the stench of my past. You're not going to attract who or what God has for you until you allow Him to deliver you from whoever or whatever has you bound. You must allow Him to make your aroma sweet for the one HE has chosen for you. I AM OUT OF THE TRASH CAN FOR GOOD, and I will not allow anything or anyone to put me back there again.

Extracted from Bishop T.D. Jakes' *New King James Bible: Woman Thou Art Loosed Edition,* page 1169:

Gospel Pearls: *"Some women have been carrying around old relationships and old experiences so long that they've become accustomed to the stench of them. God declares that thing to be dead in your life. It's time for you to bury it so you can get on with the resurrection."*

What vomit has God delivered you from? *Selah (Pause and think about that)!*

Biography

Ms. Fouchina Kirkendoll is an Amazon Best-selling author, a certified coach, motivational innovator, the recipient of the Presidential Lifetime Achievement Award, and the CEO of Chronicles of a Favored Woman, LLC in Duluth, Georgia.

Once a victim, now a survivor of sexual abuse, Ms. Kirkendoll recalls the feelings of loneliness and confusion that it caused. After decades of suffering in silence, she decided to face it head on and used the power of her voice to speak up, speak out, and to encourage others to do the same. Out of this experience is where Chronicles of a Favored Woman and its mission was birthed, to ignite the fire of one soul, one life, and one story at a time.

> "Do not give dogs what is sacred; do not throw your pearls to pigs. If you do, they may trample them under their feet, and turn and tear you to pieces."
>
> ~Matthew 7:6

Living Life to the Fullest: A Story of Passion, Perseverance, and Possibility
Omu Obilor

As the last of five children with lots of loving older cousins, my upbringing was a unique blend of sibling dynamics and extended family support. We had an extremely close-knit family filled with many traditions and rituals, including annual vacations, Sunday afternoon lunch, and holiday gatherings. These experiences created a strong sense of family identity and taught me the value of connection and community.

Despite being the youngest, I never felt like I was at a disadvantage. In fact, I was blessed to have cousins who always looked out for me and included me in their adventures. I was fortunate to have my granddad alive for several years and he instilled strong values in me that have since made a huge impact on who I am today. One of the most significant lessons I learned from my childhood experiences was the importance of perseverance and resilience. I saw how my parents and older siblings faced challenges head-on and never gave up, even in the face of adversity. This inspired me to develop a similar mindset and approach to life.

Through my story, I hope to inspire others to take risks, pursue their dreams, and never give up on their goals. So, join me as I take you along my journey and share with you the lessons learned along the way.

Looking back on my childhood, I am grateful for the love, support, and guidance I received from my family. They instilled in me the values of hard work, perseverance, and community that have stayed with me throughout my life. While my childhood wasn't perfect, it was a rich and fulfilling experience that helped shape who I am today.

In my mind's eye, it began at boarding school, where I first experienced the freedom of being away from my parents. It was a time when I learned to become more independent, but I also faced the harsh realities of living away from home. If nothing else, it taught me valuable lessons about perseverance and resilience. I begged to go as far away as possible believing it meant more pocket money for me with no one to tell me how to spend it. Little did I know what I was in for. I had money, YES, but freedom NO. During this period, I struggled with my physical appearance. I was always the tallest among my friends, and I wished I were shorter. I also thought I was too fat, and I was constantly comparing myself to others. These insecurities made it difficult for me to feel confident in social situations and affected my self-esteem.

However, winning the high school beauty pageant had a significant impact on my self-confidence. It was a huge first moment for me as I felt a sense of accomplishment and for once I didn't think my height was a disadvantage.

As I transitioned to college, I left a city I was used to, to explore new cultures and ways of life. It was a time of growth, learning, and personal development, where I mastered balancing my academics, social life, and personal goals. Now I was beginning to really understand the true meaning of independence, self-control, and setting boundaries. The freedom I had craved finally came.

Becoming a mother in 1999 was a defining moment in my life. It was a time of immense joy and overwhelming responsibility. I learned about sacrifice, unconditional love, and the strength of the human spirit. Motherhood brought with it many joys, such as seeing my son's first smile; hearing his first words and watching him take his first steps. These moments filled my heart with pride and happiness, and I knew that being a mother was the greatest role I could ever have.

However, it also came with its challenges. As a first-time mom, I was constantly worried about whether I was doing things right. I struggled with sleep deprivation, balancing work and family, and dealing with the demands of a growing child. I often felt overwhelmed and exhausted, and I didn't always know where to turn for support.

Despite these challenges, fulfilling this role has been one of the most rewarding experiences of my life. I learned the value of patience, perseverance, and sacrifice. I discovered a strength that I never knew existed. Seeing my son grow and develop into a confident and independent young man has been one of life's greatest joys. Raising him also taught me important lessons about the power of love and setting boundaries. As a parent, I learned that providing a nurturing environment while also instilling discipline and structure were essential. I also realized that it's okay to make mistakes and that being a perfect parent is non-existent.

As my son grew older, I came to understand that motherhood is a lifelong journey. Each stage of his development brought new challenges and joys, from his first words to his high school graduation. Even though he's now an adult, I'm still a proud mom who loves and supports him every step of the way.

Looking back on my experience as a mother, I'm grateful for the lessons learned and the person it has helped me become. It taught me the importance of being present, patient, and loving. It's given me a greater appreciation for the fragility and beauty of life. Motherhood has been a life-changing experience that has taught me important lessons about myself and the world around me. It's a journey that comes with its challenges, but the joys and rewards are immeasurable. I'm grateful for the opportunity of birthing my son and for the love and growth it brought into my life.

Although I had a successful tenure working at a multinational oil company, something was missing in my life. I wanted to have more control over my career and decided to take a leap of faith and pursue my passion to become an entrepreneur. Being a business owner has been a challenging and rewarding experience filled with invaluable lessons about risk-taking, resilience, and perseverance.

Leaving the comfort and stability of my job was a scary decision, but it was one of the best decisions I've ever made. Finding funding, building a team, and marketing my products and services did not come easy. However, I was driven by my determination to succeed. I learned the value of networking and building relationships with other business owners, investors, and business leaders, which helped me grow my business and expand my reach.

Another key lesson I learned was the importance of adapting to change and being flexible. As an entrepreneur, you must be able to pivot and adjust your strategy based on market conditions, customer needs, and other factors. This became evident especially in 2020, when the world came to a standstill at the hands of the Coronavirus pandemic. Although I faced many ups and downs, I never gave up on my dream. I believed in my vision, and that belief helped me to overcome the challenges and achieve success.

I'm proud of what I've accomplished and the person I've become. Deciding to become my own boss changed my life for the better and has given me a sense of purpose and fulfillment. It's an experience that I wouldn't trade for anything, and I'm grateful for the opportunity to have achieved my dreams. While filled with triumphs, joys, and sorrows, as I look back over my life, I couldn't have asked for a richer and more fulfilling experience.

As I continue along this path, I desire to continue learning, growing, and using life's lessons to make a positive impact on the world. It's a lifelong process, and there is always something new to discover and explore. Whether it's reading books, attending conferences, or taking courses, I've always tried to stay curious and open to diverse ideas and perspectives. It has also helped me stay relevant and adaptable in an ever-changing world. Another integral part of my journey is expressing gratitude. It keeps me grounded and connected to my values and priorities. It has also helped me cultivate deeper relationships with the people around me and to see the world through a more positive and hopeful lens.

Something that I hold near and dear to my heart is working with children living with cancer. I currently serve on the Board of Directors of Children Living with Cancer Foundation, and I'm committed to helping these children and their families cope with the challenges it brings. Every child deserves a chance to live a happy and healthy life, and I'm excited about doing my part to make that a reality.

One of my future aspirations is to start a soup kitchen to help the less privileged. Everyone deserves access to nutritious food and hunger should not be a barrier to living a happy and fulfilling life. I hope to provide a safe and welcoming space for people in need of access to healthy food and who desire to belong and feel a part of their community.

I have no doubt that my future is filled with endless opportunities for personal growth and development. I aspire to live a life that is true to my values and priorities and are aligned with my deepest beliefs and convictions. I'm filled with a sense of excitement and anticipation and know that with hard work, perseverance, and a positive outlook, the sky's the limit.

From the joys and challenges of motherhood to the risks and rewards of entrepreneurship, to my desire to help children with cancer and the less privileged, my journey continues to be a wild and wonderful ride. But the story is far from over! There are still many adventures to be had, challenges to overcome, and future dreams to pursue. So stay tuned for the next chapter, there's so much more to share. Until then, let's keep living with passion, purpose, and excitement, for the best is yet to come!

Biography

Ms. Omu Obilor is a transformational leadership expert who delivers high-energy keynote presentations that challenge audiences to leverage their values and pay attention to what matters most at work and in life. Attendees love her practical strategies that are applicable personally and professionally.

She has a knack for making meaningful connections with everyone she comes in contact with and an insatiable appetite for helping others maximize their potential. Ms. Obilor knows how to rock a platform, connect with the crowd, and provide invaluable training so that others can effectively do the same.

Her down-to-earth humor compels audiences to laugh while they learn. She engages groups from the moment she steps into the room and leaves them with empowering tools and focused mindsets that they will use long after the event's lights have gone out. She is passionate about people, leadership, and successful businesses and is especially inspired to help people take their careers – and themselves – to unprecedented levels.

A founding member of the John Maxwell Team, Ms. Obilor is also a neuroencoding specialist, TEDx speaker, as well as the Executive Director and National Trainer for Business Network International (BNI) among other organizations, where she leverages her neurolinguistic programming and brain health certifications to create groundbreaking transformations.

She has spoken about various issues on diverse world stages based on her extensive expertise. She is an Executive Contributor to *Brainz Magazine,* a global digital publication featuring exclusive interviews, informative articles, and information on entrepreneurship, personal development, leadership and lifestyle.

Ms. Obilor has been trained and mentored by some of the world's best such as Les Brown, Joseph McClendon III, Paul Martinelli, John Maxwell, and Ivan Misner. As an international speaker, she has spoken at various international conferences and summits globally, including the Neuroencoding Institute Conference in Las Vegas, BNI global team workshops, and several others.

A Board Member of the non-profit organization Children Living With Cancer Foundation, she has touched the lives of children and families with children living with cancer. Whilst mentoring women and young girls through her executive position on the Global Women Connect and Global Give Back Circle respectively, Ms. Obilor lives, plays, and works in Lagos, Nigeria, working alongside her world-class team who are just as committed to helping people achieve success as much as she is.

> "If you don't like something, change it.
> If you can't change it, change your attitude."
> ~ Maya Angelou

Breaking all the Rules
Lisa Dove Washington

Have you ever felt that you were just not good enough, or that you didn't meet the standards of most? Have you ever felt like no matter how you showed up in the world and no matter how hard you tried, it never seemed to be enough for others, family and friends included? I know I have, and for me, that has been a cross to bear for many years. I am guilty as charged in the area of trying to please others to no avail. It drains and weighs you down in a way that makes life difficult and even depressing at times. It can even make you feel imperfect, right? I know better than most! But I am going to challenge your thinking by suggesting that not only are "imperfections" OK, but they also reveal a fierceness that many work hard to obtain while also providing a focus on life that is as close to "PERFECT" as you can get! Let me explain.

Having imperfections are a great thing because they allow you space to grow. Growth pushes you closer towards healing, and healing allows you to embrace your truth. As a result, you find peace in knowing who you are and are able to clearly focus on the good while identifying the areas that need more attention, it's what I like to call the "push through" mindset. That to me is the true definition of fierceness. In no way am I suggesting that the journey is easy, but I am suggesting that it is a journey worth taking.

Over the years, I have grown to understand that it is ok to embrace my imperfections, but that is not the way my journey started. I always felt like I had to please people in order to get them to respect and like me, which was very important to me. I was very accommodating of a lot of things that weren't necessarily in my best interest, and I took chances in life that I now look back and say, "Thank you, God for keeping me." I know that if it wasn't for Him, I might not even be here today. I am sure we all have had those moments, but what makes this a key part of the journey is the recognition and acknowledgement of it.

When I was a young mother, while attending college simultaneously, I struggled, not just because I had a baby, but because I felt like I had disappointed so many people in my life. I knew that juggling my pregnancy and college was just asking for a life of hardship. By no means was it easy and there were many who thought I was headed down the wrong path. Success had become an anomaly for me and something that I would probably never run across in life. It appeared that everyone thought it was doomsday for me. And I must admit, in their eyes, and in mine, I had broken all the rules that most people follow who want to become somebody in life and live productively. I watched other people follow those rules to the "T" while I spiraled into depression many times because not only was I disappointing my family and friends, but I was also disappointing GOD! I knew that this was not the life He intended for me. It was my fault, and I deserved to experience the lack of confidence that many had in me. And when I tell you it was hard, that doesn't even halfway explain it. I struggled getting up on time for class and on some days didn't go at all because now I had a little one to get ready too. I struggled with finding someone I could trust and afford to care for her while I continued to further my education. Not only that, but I also couldn't afford the things that I needed to take care of my precious cargo. You know, the basics. I needed gas for my car to take her to daycare and get me to school, not to mention the money required to pay for daycare, food, and other necessities. Being a student with a baby was simply not conducive to being able to purchase those things, at least not with ease.

Now I am not suggesting that I did not have help. My mom was right there with me, helping me at every turn. But for those who know all too well about that thing called "PRIDE," whew, I carried that thing higher than the clouds above! Taking care of my baby was my responsibility and no one else's. I had to figure this out on my own and didn't want to burden anyone along the way, and at the very least, avoid depending on others as much as possible. I had the wherewithal to understand that bringing a child into this world was going to be one hell of a feat. Was I discouraged at times? Yes! Was I scared half to death? I was absolutely terrified! But one thing I can also say is, I was determined! Determined to do it, no matter what! Yes, I had a false image or perception of how huge the task would be, but I was determined to figure it out, and "Focus" became my middle name!

But guess what was the first thing I had to do? I had to drop my "PRIDE" and to me, that was one of the hardest things I ever had to do. As much as I wanted to raise my little girl on my own, because I did not want to burden anyone else, the truth is, I needed help. That was truly tough for me. I had to allow myself to become vulnerable, while eating a piece of humble pie to ask for and accept help from others. I had to accept the fact that I just couldn't do it alone. So, I did. I reached out to friends who loved and supported me and asked if they would babysit while I went to work. Yes, I also worked while attending college, and had to ask my mom if she would assist with picking my daughter up from daycare or putting her to sleep at night if I had to work late. Understand, I could not assume that she could or would, but I had no other choice than to ask her. Although that was hard for me, I had to do it, not just for me, but for my daughter. That was the selflessness that I had to come to grips with. It was not just about me and my feelings, but this was about allowing the village to be there and guide me to a place where I in fact could do more on my own.

That was a moment of truth, when I realized that although I had made some decisions that led me on a path that would cause me to regroup and re-focus, the determination to keep going had also been instilled in me. My imperfections played a pivotal role in my growth where I learned to trust others and accepted the fact that it was ok and even necessary at times to simply "ASK" for help. No one can get to any place of significance alone and that concept has helped me to understand and embrace what being fierce and focused are really all about!

But in life, the lessons never stop, right? If you don't think that's true, then just keep on living! There is always room to know better so you can do better. I would have many lessons to learn after college while raising my daughter. Yet, I still struggled with feeling as though I was disappointing those closest to me. The pressure was unspoken but very real. Remember, not only did I conceive a child while in college, I also wasn't married! That was a whole different can of worms. It was a heaviness that I continued to carry. And this was a true disappointment because in the book of rules, to me, this was one of the biggest rules to break, ever. I believed that I would never be forgiven for this one, no matter how much I had done right, or how much I had overcome. In my eyes, I was still a failure and disappointment, and this was on a much bigger scale! To add insult to injury, I had become so overwhelmed with everything – getting my education, working, and raising a child – that I was not working to my best potential. I was spreading myself thin. I had to decide what my next moves were going to be because my journey shifted and unfortunately, after attending college for five years, I had to walk away. Unfortunately, I struggled to maintain a good GPA and could no longer juggle everything and still make it. As a result, I had to make a grown-up decision for my daughter and me and get a job to take care of us. However, I had not taken college completely off the table, but I knew I had to set it aside and switch my focus to my child, who was now my first priority. Although difficult, there was no other choice to make.

Having a child out of wedlock was a "no-no" in everyone's book as far as I was concerned. I would have loved to have gotten married before I had a child, and that is what I had hoped for, but things didn't work out that way. No excuses, it just didn't work out that way because of my decisions. I own that. More importantly, I also knew that God was not happy with this and that caused me turmoil for years. While I was grateful and appreciative of my mom's support and love every step of the way, as well as the support from some of my friends and family, but the one thing I couldn't shake was what God thought about me? I already feared disappointing others, but disappointing God was so much more and something I never wanted to do, and yet, I felt like I did that on such a huge level.

For the most part, I truly believed I was a good person inside and out, but the struggle was why others didn't see it? Why would the imperfection of lacking the willpower to say "NO" be attached to me, especially in a situation that drastically changed my life? To make matters worse, it was also a sin in the eyes of God. What was wrong with me? Clearly I knew better but didn't do better. I saw that as a huge imperfection. I had lost focus on what was important -- to be the best I could be. Although it was important for me to be a good mom, I felt I was disappointing my own child because I brought her into this world and had already begun creating a life filled with continuous challenges and struggles. Getting married was always a part of my future, yet I had feelings of not being good enough. Because I had already "broken the rules," I felt as if I had nothing to bring to the table. So why would anyone find me worthy of marriage at this point. It was a never-ending spiral of negative thoughts and emotions that often leads to additional missteps in life. Think about it, I had a college education, was raised in a family of professionals who worked hard for their money and were great examples in our community, and here I was, putting a blemish on my family's legacy. The nerve, right?

But the one thing that carried me through this part of my journey was having a "push through" mindset. I had to shift my focus on what was good while identifying what needed my attention! Consistency is key and when you find what works, you keep pushing. My heart was in the right place, that was a plus. Providing my daughter with the best life possible was a plus. Although difficult, deciding to take a break from college to focus on my responsibilities was a huge plus. But never being proposed to and saying, "I Do," was a minus for me. Even though I was determined to focus on the good, that one negative outweighed EVERYTHING! However I dug deep and prayed every step of the way, asking for advice and direction from the same people who helped me in the past. I eventually accepted the fact that while some of my decisions took me off of the original path that my parents and others set for me, God had bigger plans. What I know to be true is, He never brings you to anything that he doesn't intend to bring you through. Even though I thought breaking all the rules would be my downfall, it provided me the strength to tackle anything that came my way. I was given this path for a reason, and it has taught me so much about who I am and who I am called to be. Life is a journey of lessons, blessings, failing, making mistakes, and sometimes even breaking the rules. Whether it's on purpose or not it's the journey you were meant to be on.

God is faithful! I have accomplished things that I thought I never would or even dreamed of. Everything I told myself that I didn't deserve because of my missteps and mistakes, has come full circle. It just goes to show you that whatever you imagine yourself doing pales in comparison to what God has in store for you. It is all about what you do while on your journey. Your choices matter! I love my imperfections NOW, because they have contributed to many of the opportunities that have been afforded to me.

In a nutshell, I'm grateful for my imperfections because they have helped shape me into the woman I am today. Even when I had those moments of feeling less than and making poor decisions, little did I know that God was turning them for my good. He turned my messes into miracles and gave me a pair of fresh eyes so I could see that my mistakes were just a part of the journey. God has blessed me with a solid foundation from which to build on to learn and grow. Today, I am stronger and wiser, and I have life's challenges and hurdles to thank. I'm no longer ashamed to show my "scars" because they allowed me to become vulnerable so I could share my story with others. They also have made me fierce beyond compare and provided me with a laser focus to complete my assignment. Life is what you make it, but you must be open to learn all that it's trying to teach you. That's what having a growth mindset is all about. Never let anyone discourage you from becoming a life-long learner. So don't ever stop trying and no matter what, never give up.

If you have learned anything from what I have shared in this chapter or experienced anything close to what I have gone through, first let me say, you are not alone. There is always someone who understands your plight and struggles, and it's ok. But let me suggest that there is no such thing as perfection unless you are embracing your imperfections. It's your imperfections that make you unique and fearfully and wonderfully made. That is a level of strength that most don't even know they possess let alone tap into. So with that being said, I give you the key to embrace your imperfectly fierce and focused self and rise above your imperfections and crush every goal. Unlock that door that has been holding you back and push through it. There is greatness waiting for you on the other side, and when you get there, you won't be alone because there will be others waiting for you. They just took different paths that's all. You got this! It's goal crushing time!

Biography

Known for her wit, candor, and passion, **Lisa Dove Washington** is an author, speaker, journalist, magazine publisher, and event host. A Washington, D.C. native, her connection to the local community rivals many. Whether she's volunteering with a girl's mentorship program or hosting a product launch party with D.C.'s finest, her gift of gab and contagious energy set the mood of the room.

A proud graduate of the District's Howard D. Woodson Sr. High School and Atlanta's Spelman College respectively, Mrs. Washington and her family support educational and social activities throughout DC, Maryland, and

Virginia, affectionately known as the DMV. She consistently keeps her communication skills sharp, as the host and creator of the online show, "Lunchin' with Lisa," (www.lunchinwithlisa.com) which streams LIVE every Thursday on Facebook and YouTube, as well as Founder and CEO of *Dove Style Magazine* (www.dovestylemagazine.org), an online publication. Another part of her repertoire includes Touched By a Dove Publishing (www.touchedbyadovepublishing.com), that she launched in 2019.

To learn more about Lisa Dove Washington's upcoming schedule and published works, *The Power of Shut Up, Unleash Your Superpower, 6 Extraordinary Stories on Discovering & Accepting The Power Within,* and *When Gigi Meets Kam: The Unyielding Love of a Grandmother*; or if you need a moderator, speaker, storyteller, or event host at your next event, go to www.lisadovewashington.com for more information.

To Conclude the Whole Matter...

We know all too well that when we get in our own way, we run the chance of limiting our success and stunting our progress. It's very easy to tell ourselves why we cannot do something or aren't worthy of happiness, prosperity, or good health. However, I hope that by reading *Imperfectly Fierce & Focused: Rising Above Your Imperfections While Still Crushing Your Goals*, you have now gained a different perspective about challenges and how to deal with them. I pray that at least one of the co-authors resonated with you and you've committed to implement their tips and strategies as you continue along life's journey.

Remember these lasting words of encouragement:

Even in the worst situations, you can still grow from it and through it. Life is about perspective. No matter how bad it gets, something good can still come out of it. So look at your challenges and face them head on. That is the beginning of healing and growth.

You deserve happiness and joy despite the mistakes you've made. I know because I have made plenty. You're worthy of having peace of mind. So seek those things that bring you happiness, joy and peace, and lean into them. Never allow anyone to hold your past over your head in an attempt to make you feel guilty. Learn to forgive yourself, as well as those who have hurt you, then release it all.

And lastly, acknowledge every win that you've accomplished – big or small. Take time to celebrate it all. Why? Because it will help you to keep going until you reach your goal! It is important to keep your accomplishments in the forefront of your mind. It is very easy to get lost in the translations of life, relationships, and business. We get so engrossed in what has and is happening in our lives that we lose sight of how far we have come. So acknowledge your progress. Celebrate yourself and know that it's okay to make mistakes. But when you make them, learn from them, grow from them, and move on. It's progress over perfection! All milestones in life, relationships, and business MATTER!

Always remember...nothing is wasted in the end. All things work together for your good!

Keever Lernise Murdaugh
Visionary Author

www.ingramcontent.com/pod-product-compliance
Lightning Source LLC
Chambersburg PA
CBHW071858070526
44583CB00016B/1751